MW01503915

FLIGHTS, FREEWAYS AND DETOURS

(Of Vacations and Travel)

By: Shirley Ensrud

Shirley Ensrud

CONTENTS

LOCAL TRAVEL

GO WEST, YOUNG MAN

TO THE SUNSHINE STATE

TO NEW ENGLAND AND BEYOND

WORLD TRAVEL

For Deb
my daughter who,
as a teacher,
opens new worlds
for elementary children

Foreword

Every experience is an opportunity
for expanding horizons. In this book
we look especially at travel and vacation
adventures.
We have sampled bountiful USA, a small
area of Europe and a bit of Canada.
There is so much more to encounter
in our Golden Years
that this collection
may never be completed.

LOCAL TRAVEL

SAVORING SUMMER

We leave fertile, flat, black soil
planted with corn and beans
to find at the river town
hills, rocks, trees.

Between, a ribbon of concrete—
monument to our need
to get there fast.

Scent of skunk affronts nostrils;
later, fragrance of fresh peas
as combines move down rows.

Mobile home surrounded by a new grove
of poplars is contradiction to eyes
conditioned to rambling farmhouses
with random cottonwoods.

Tents, trailers and outdoor grills
dot a campground with pool and golf course,
alive with children in brief suits,
adults with sticks hitting balls.

A stand of native oak remains
untouched, unmowed.

Thoreau would scoff at us
speeding through the countryside,
but we are observing.

NIGHT ADVENTURE

I am alone in the universe except for
other mavericks, their headlights
twin stars diffused by rain.
An airport beacon revolves
in anticipated arcs, sweeps the blackness.
Broken strings of rhinestones
have rolled to the horizon,
illuminators of farmers' dooryards.

Roadsigns, mile markers, telephone poles
appear upside-down in wet paving;
eerie luminescence hovers over villages.

Brightness rises eastward as orange buses
steal along, stop at designated places,
ingest school children. In half-light, trees,
barns, silos silhouette against pink sky.

Loath to leave behind that ethereal place
and my own seclusion, I forge into daytime.

TWILIGHT IN THE COUNTRY

We absorb ambiance
as brittle corn leaves become gold
in slanting rays of sun.
Slight breeze turns them
to quivering witch fingers.

Light glows on undersides of clouds,
edges them with silver.
Trees in fence lines cast long shadows;
holsteins tread crooked paths to barns.

A paintbrush might better
describe the picture, though neither
painter nor poet can capture for another
the surge of emotion in the breast.

HEIGHTENED AWARENESS

Tour a restored turn-of-the century theater,
imagine the whisper of long skirts,
see buckled spats on shoes, feel the breeze
from programs waving before faces
in opera house not air conditioned.

Envy this town the cherubs and gold leaf,
curving stairways with polished railings,
pillared and covered entry where once
gentlemen and ladies alighted.

So much from that era is gone; besides
demolishing ornate buildings, we have
lost much of the formality and respect.
Oh, that we might consider carefully
before committing to change.

OCTOBER OUTING

Soybean seedpods cling
to nearly nude stems;
ears of corn hang down, heavy.
Cultivated fields divide
around scraggly stands of oak that,
 in turn, are sliced by winding streams.

Horses trot in pastures, tails flying.
Herefords and jerseys idle in meadows
as farmers spread manure on fields.

Bluffs are a Monet of colored leaves.
Birds erupt from ditches,
swirl, dip as a single body,
black the sky–then almost disappear
on certain turns.
Occasional windmills creak.

Why do we embark on foreign travel
when all this is a half-day drive
from where we live?

3

MALL OF AMERICA

A non-entity on a courtesy bench,
I am surrounded by shopping bags
full of treasures left by daughters
gone opposite directions
on one more quest.

Uncaring as well as unaware
of my observation pass before me
individuals, families, busloads of humanity
dressed in saris, sweat shirts, bib overalls,
wild animal prints; their tummies
showing, faces painted, heads shaved
or hair dyed purple.

They carry video cameras,
cell phones, jackets, clipboards,
bulging paper bags or Mall totes;
snack on orange julius,
pizza, donuts, cinnabuns;
push strollers with infants giggling,
sleeping or crying, carry children on backs
or shoulders, maneuver wheelchairs.

There is Snoopy's red dish, larger
than the stock-watering tank of my childhood,
and the Red Baron himself, two stories high;
at right, four-story Lego Imagination Center
with automated dinosaurs surrounded
by play stations for hands-on fun
and between, a ferris wheel and roller coaster
carry screaming passengers.

Whole shops are devoted to earrings,
neckties or glassware. Kiosks offer
everything from tee shirts with rude imprints
to hand-blown angels and unicorns.

Shoppers go from carnival atmosphere
of eat stands and noisy rides
into sanctuary of muted lighting
and piano music in department stores
with New York names.

4

Tourists come by plane to be shuttled here
to play, to eat, to shop, to see
living creatures in an aquarium,
to be able to say they have been here.

The pulse of the place is frenetic
as they try to experience it all in four hours,
though they cannot.

GRANDCHILDREN OF THE PRAIRIE

Thirty-story buildings connected
by telephone wires and fax machines
collect secretaries, CEOs and salespersons,
send them skyward in carpeted boxes.

They, two generations removed
from farmland stretching horizontally,
will vie for parking places,
schools for their children, housing,
and not understand the concept
of giving a hand in a barn raising.

PROGRESS GONE BERSERK?

"Eminent Domain," they cite,
condemn farmland,
surround cities with concrete frames

but suburbs tumble out beyond them
like fluff from dandelions;
first townhouses and McDonalds,
then golf courses and malls.

How long will it be
before the need to plant potatoes
on the number nine green?

ADVICE FOR SMALL-TOWN SENIORS IN THE CITY

Turn left, then right from the elevator,
poke plastic card into a slot to gain entrance,
draw curtains for foreign panorama two hours from home...
not foreign as in other country, but nearly other-worldly.
Look down on rooftops that are parking lots,
up at buildings taller yet than where you stay,
across at Center where professionals play games
and pedestrians and cars clog the street.
Watch neon words chase across signs,
matchbox-size vehicles flow through intersections,
snake over and around highways at three levels.

See reflections of other edifices waver
in glass-sided skyscraper across the way.
Car lights come on as sun settles, become
white centipedes arriving, red ones retreating.
Appreciate square architecture of recent constructions
that complements round-topped windows of elders,
a half-block mural on lower level of gray building,
Coca Cola sign a whole story high.

Go down to ground level, stroll, try not to stare
at ethnicity, street people, youth hanging around.
Enter shops where prices frighten pocketbooks,
hold elbows to your sides in china department,
gape at multiplicity of choices–color, size, design,
smile at neckties pricier than your first three-piece suit.

Ignore cost of entrees and enjoy,
even though your recipe is just as good.
Remember to tip. Carry half-meal in a box
to store in refrigerator at weekend home in the sky.
Brew coffee in In-Room service,
lounge on sofa to watch "Wheel of Fortune."
Enjoy good seats in splendor of renovated theater,
remember to thank offspring who reserved
all this for you, picked up the tab.

Sleep well.
Don't make the bed.

PANORAMA AT TWILIGHT

Pink watercolor wash spreads
over eastern vista ahead;
color lifts, horizon darkens.
Above and sides turn melon-colored.
Vees of geese, stitches in the sky
add sound to an otherwise quiet ,
like youth forging into the future.

A single dot of light which seems
a plane refuses to move, proves it is,
indeed a star–as in middle age
we strive for steadiness.

Rear-view mirror reflects sky
paling to aqua, jet streams
sparkle white on fuchsia clouds;
trees, barns, silos become silhouettes.
In senior years, much of the loveliness
is in the looking back and remembering.

FROM ST. PETER TO MANKATO

Between an erratic branch
of the Minnesota River
and bluffs clothed in jewel tones–
ruby, garnet, amber, gold, bronze
in sumac, bushes and weeds
interspersed with jade of trees
not yet turned, we find plots
of partly harvested farmland
with its own charm in stubble
of gleaned crops, black
chisel-plowed fields
and distinctive dry yellow
of corn ready for combine
that one can nearly hear.

A shiny, green, 1939 Chevy
Caprice convertible, top down, passes...
claims spouse's attention.

STURDY AND/OR FREE

A thundering waterfall
gives impetus
to the river's headlong plunge
to the sea.
Over rocks, past trees,
it cannot be denied
its adventure.

Leaves flutter down,
bob and pirouette on the water;
forsake a rainbow in the mist,
an aspen on shore.

Some of us stay with the tree
while others float with leaves;
each wondering if those
have the fuller existence.

THE PAMPERED LIFE

I tour Caribbean isles
via Cruise Line, drive a Porsche
to Country Clubs
and snow-covered skiing hills
with scattered aspens,
wear a Pendleton jacket,
my escort clad by Giorgio Armani
(though I should ask him
to change his hairstyle.)

I peek at my Rolex
to see if we will arrive at
the Intercontinental Hotel
in time to sip Remy Martin
from Waterford crystal.

I visit exotic places
between the covers
of glossy magazines.

GO WEST, YOUNG MAN

FIRST FLIGHT

Up here
I realize how small I am
and you are
and presidents and kings and even armies are!

Up here
cities look like villages,
highways like threads,
and fields, quilt pieces.

Sea and sky meld
into oneness of brilliant blue
as far as eye can see.
Sometimes, a haze of clouds on the horizon
is the only separation.

Cloud structures below
change constantly and magically,
at times appear to be:
    icing on a cake
    cotton balls
    hard, crusty snowbanks
    a white Grand Canyon
    pebbles in a stream
    storybook castles

Sometimes we are enshrouded in clouds
and cannot see tip of wings.
Moments later we burst into sunshine.

Likely never again will I be so overcome
with such sensory perceptions
nor my own insignificance
as today.

THROUGH BLUE SKY

Thirty-five thousand feet
above our anxious nation,
a nearly full 757 attests
that we will not be
intimidated by terrorists.

Determined to show the world
our lives go on,
we fly across the U.S.
to celebrate a birthday;
munch pretzels, savor coffee–
the only nourishment provided
soon after September eleventh.

With hazy clouds below,
a round spot of rainbow winks
as if reflected from a prism;
a jewel, a temporary gift.

The plane turns, sun reflects
off the wing and the rainbow
is on the page of my book.
I accept the promise.

SOUTH DAKOTA, 2001

West of Chamberlain mounds rise and fall,
greener this year than most, with ponds in low spots.
Near streams, tenacious trees shelter far-scattered houses.

We climb to where green meets blue at horizon
with no obstruction; no tree, no building...
just road signs and planted trees for snow fences.

Beyond wild grasses lie tilled fields,
beef cattle fenced in, hay bales.
Billboards announce food, amusements,
Wall Drug, Badlands, Corn Palace.

Interstate ninety leads past deserted homesteads.
Grain bins dot fields with no obvious owner.
Brown fallow fields bisect thousands of acres of wheat.
Grain elevators and water towers rise above villages.

Angus with cavorting calves huddle
in the corner of a hillside pasture.

It feels lonesome to me,
but my friend back home
who lived through dust storms here
still yearns for it all.

IMPRESSIONS OF MONTANA

Asphalt undulates through yellow sweet clover,
sagebrush, strip farming, occasional windmills,
abandoned buildings, flowering yucca, rock
and nature-planted trees that seem stunted
compared to oaks at home.

Low-slung mountains, a medley of green and brown,
are broken only by railroad tracks, rows of tall crosses
carrying electricity and wires strung between posts.
Gates at roads leading to ranches beyond hills are closed.

Along lesser roads, crooked sticks hold up sagging fences;
beside freeway, no-nonsense-U. S. of A. treated posts
keep woven wire stretched taut.

Hazy clouds float, wispy enough to filter
but not obliterate sun; promise no rain.
Farther west, prosperous crop farms
boast oil wells in wheat fields,
straw bales stacked in pyramids
six wide and a half-block long
and well-tended homesteads.

Sun peeks through cumulus clouds,
highlights certain areas like a blessing.

FROM NOTES SCRIBBLED IN IDAHO

High desert, big sky, tan soil, sagebrush,
potatoes, alfalfa, wheat, flat, straight highway,
snow-capped mountains, irrigation, canals,
beef cattle on open range, dairy farms, hay bales.

Enjoyment of other is real
after several trips west by plane.

ON A SIDE TRIP OFF THE HIGHWAY

Teens the size of postage stamps
stand on a bridge that spans the chasm,
wave to their mother beside me.
Centered in her view finder,
they pace before water
free-falling from unseen source
hundreds of feet to a ledge,
then misting down
to a basin below and behind them.
The photo will be two girls
and a small section of the falls.
Man with camcorder
captures it all in wide lens.

The sheer size and poetry
of its undulations
and music of its roar at bottom
diminish our significance.

I retrace the path down man-made steps
that drew me there.
Stream gurgles beside, over rocks,
through culvert under bridge,
out into the Columbia.
Undergrowth, moss-covered trees,
ripening berries frame it all
and diminutive black and white birds
the size of my thumb flit
from twig to limb,
give another dimension.

BOTH SIDES OF THE MOUNTAIN

Under cloudy skies, leave Fresno
on multi-level, curved freeways
through vineyards, orchards,
fields of pistachios, kiwi, kumquats,
avocados, artichokes.
Roadside stands sell produce.
Gilroy has garlic ice cream.

Tumbleweeds, scrub brush
cover the east side of coastal range
where left to nature.
Canal water from mountain-top
sprinkles, drips or is furrowed
between rows.
Holsteins cover acres on dairy farms,
emus, ostrich, llamas
survive in smaller spaces.

Fog settles before the mountain pass;
at apex, sunshine.
The road twists, climbs and descends between
moss-covered rocks and gnarly oaks,
then down to blacker soil.
Some medians retain flowering bushes
though cement replaces most.

Sound barriers line freeways
at San Francisco.
Hotels and missions reflect
Spanish architecture.
Palm trees line some streets,
eucalyptus, like naked warriors,
guard others.

In less than an afternoon,
experience the dichotomy of California.

OVERNIGHT IN CALIFORNIA STATE PARK

Redwoods high as skyscrapers
surround a stump the size of my kitchen,
rise from its roots.
Reflectors on tree trunks deflect vehicles
from scraping bark, and roads
curve around reigning giants.

Tops of trees from bottom
of gorge at left are eye level
and long-stemmed daisies
edge dense forest on right.

Secluded by undergrowth between sites,
neighbors erect tents,
children ride bicycles on paths
or tiptoe on stones across a stream.
Towels and wet suits hang
from makeshift lines.
A bluejay perches on our picnic table.

We read while daylight lingers,
go to sleep in our RV as youth
next door picks tunes on his guitar

AN EXERCISE IN FAITH

All manner of vehicles vie for space
on four lanes each way, 60 miles per hour,
drivers eating sandwiches,
holding cell phone conversations,
funneling into traffic from ramps,
confident they will be given place.
Flicks of light announce lane changes.

Orange-jacketed man holds "SLOW" sign,
sends traffic to single file. Crews
at our mercy rebuild, repair, perspire
as we zoom within inches of their bodies.
After the last orange barrels we accelerate,
go back out and resume the skirmish.

14

OVERHEARD IN CAFE OUT WEST

"Going with me in the morning?"
"Would if I had the money."
"Won't cost much. Leaving at 3:30.
Be in Vegas by noon."

"Didn't think you gambled."
"Don't. Getting cheap motel,
watching the game. Can't get it here."
"Oh, I can see that, then.
Wouldn't gamble myself."

He sits back,
lights another cigarette.

WHEN YOU STOP AT RENO

Pull gold-plated handle on all-glass door
and step into fantasy world; be duplicated
in mirrors on all sides.

Silver dollars clang into trays,
nickels tinkle, lights twinkle,
bells and whistles add to the clangor.

Women in shorts, skirts, halters,
pants, dresses wear fanny packs
like badges, carry cups to hold winnings,
move from machine to machine
like farmers from field to field,
or stake claim to one paying off
until prize is all fed back.

Bow-tied young men stand
at crescent-shaped tables surrounded
by men perched on high stools wearing
boots, hats, jeans, tees or business suits
making scraping motions for one more card.
Dealer flicks them out, smiles, rakes in chips.

To be certain of winning, eat at the buffet.

THROUGH UTAH IN A DAY

At western edge of Utah
on early August day
we enter an RV park,
retire at sun's last ray.

The wind sets up a howl,
our bed rocks to and fro.
Tent campers take their blankets
to car or van and stow

away to hope for let-up
that's not about to be.
In morning upon rising
we all get up to see

if there's extensive damage;
surprisingly, there's not.
We go back into traffic.
The day is very hot.

First scene that we encounter
is desert, white and flat.
For miles we see no other;
roadway is good through that.

The choir in Salt Lake City
is pride of Morman folk.
The majesty of mountains
surrounds it like a cloak.

Tour book states beef and dairy
are agriculture core.
They flourish far from freeway
where Zane Gray set his lore.

We've not time for the side trip
to forest, park and plain.
We vow to do it one day
when we pass here again.

WHO KNOWS WHAT RICHES

Rural Nevada looks worthless
to mid-westerners.
Busy railroad and long, level freeway
follow Humboldt river basin
through miles of sagebrush
under cloudless sky.
Narrow roads lead off to oblivion.

With four ranges of mountains on horizon
we think, "What wasteland,"
until tour book reference
advises those hills are harvested
of gold, silver, tungsten, mercury,
opals and turquoise.

COWBOY'S LAMENT
(Written at Elko, Nevada,
"Home of Cowboy Poetry")

As I look about
at the bare terrain
and my mouth and throat
are dry

I see clouds afar
that may drop some rain
on the mount's far side–
I sigh.

We just ride and rope
as we wait in vain
for a change in the tone
of sky

but there's nowhere else
(though I do complain)
where I'd rather live
or die.

17

FROM PHOENIX TO TUCSON AT DUSK

Yellow emanates from west peak,
east clouds spread out,
turn pink as inside of seashells.
Soon, purple-tinted, scant
western clouds blush lilac, fuchsia;
portend no rain for brown soil
cleared of cacti, disced smooth.

Every-colored cumulus dissipate,
allow orange sun-glow radiation.
Palm trees, cholla, prickly pear
show green at roadside.
Far mountains form silhouettes,
as if a child with scissors
had cut a rendition of horizon.

Sky pales, east clouds fade, others
are briefly red, then nondescript.
Overhead dome becomes silver/gray
before starshine.

One nearly expect credits
to roll across the screen.

ANCIENT CITY CAFE

Forty miles from anyplace
Indian woman hurries,
takes orders, delivers meals.
Straight, black hair to her waist,
Nikes on her feet, girl clears tables,
fills coffee cups.
Scandinavian lady in kitchen
cooks, fries, arranges plates
assisted by blonde,
male giant in shorts.

Tall, stick-thin cowboys in black hats,
jeans torn at the knees,
order tortillas and iced tea.
Artsy couple,
faces framed in long white hair–
she in velvet garb, he wearing a beret–
take a table by the window.

Food is good, coffee just fifty cents,
ambiance something not found
in franchise places.

TEXAS PANHANDLE

Blue road signs, green mile markers
the only splashes of color
along twin strips of highway
splitting far-reaching tan soil
veined by wandering dry creek beds;
here and there, oil wells,
occasional green plots of crops,
a rest area in a domed hill.

Semis surround gas stations with cafes
on outskirts of metro
that might be in any state
with the requisite fast-food places
and motels–Amarillo.

Again crops, windmills, flatland,
the only hills manmade bridges
over other roads.
Scent of manure draws our eyes
to acres of stockyards
and red-soiled bush-covered buttes.

Who says it takes all day to cross Texas?

SIGNPOST

We cross the Platte, barely 10 ft. wide, 8" deep.
    "Too thin to plow,
    Too thick to drink."

MEMORIAL TO GOVERNMENT BUILDING
NO LONGER THERE

Voices haunt me:
presidents, children, spiritual leaders,
newscasters, families, survivors,
those dying; a cacophony on tape
as we move from room to room.

Blatant visuals:
shattered eyeglasses, windows, computers,
rubble, twisted file drawers, child's T-shirt,
crumpled appointment books,
photos of each victim encased in glass.

    Mothers dropped children at daycare
    Men met for prayer breakfast
    Secretaries answered phones
    Executives organized days
    At 9:02 their world exploded

Outside, 168 empty chairs,
bronze and glass in nine rows,
one for each floor.
A chair for each person killed
with 19 of them smaller,
remembering children.

An 80-year-old elm survived,
now encircled by a stone
promontory inscribed:
    "The spirit of this city and this nation
    will not be defeated..."

A half-inch skim of water flows
over black granite
saved from the rubble–
soothes, calms.

Viewers snap photos, walk quietly,
reverently.

YELLOWSTONE FOREST FIRE

Clouds billow and roll, mass, grow dense;
lightning zig-zags, touches dry grass.
Underbrush ignites, then twigs, branches.
A whole tree blazes, then another.

Fire escalates, fed by pine needles.
Smoke sends burrowing animals below ground,
fowl to flight, large creatures to prairie or river.
Insects perish; eggs, deep within trunks, survive.

Humans come with picks, shovels, water, foam,
helicopters. Blaze persists,
blacks thousands of acres of public lands.
Blanket of snow puts out fire in single night.

Foraging animals must eat pine needles;
the old, weak and very young perish.
Carnivores and scavengers eat well.

Old Faithful and other thermals
pour steaming water into streams.
Herbivores graze shorelines,
ducks swim on warm ponds.

Dormant grasses, wildflowers spring forth,
replace sagebrush, green the meadows.
Deer, bear, bison
that weathered the winter return.

Rains wash sediments from ashes into rivers.
Plankton flourish to feed mussels and insects
which nourish fish, birds and animals.

Carpenter ants pillage fallen trunks.
Bees move into their tunnels, begin pollinating.
Seeds released from cones
bring forth seedlings that will be trees,
will, again, be forests.

THERE ARE THREE WYOMINGS

Mountains, buttes, long trains,
cranes at mining venture,
antelope, range cattle, sagebrush slopes.

Flatlands, snaky narrow streams,
dry riverbeds, cloudless sky,
woven wire fences, oil wells, sheep.

Hay bales, wheat, strip farming,
irrigation, corn, sunflowers.

This third reminds us
we will soon be home.

KANSAS CAFÉ

Drive Highway 54
through brown ditches and meadowland
dotted with leftover snow.

Stop at Phil's 54 Diner
with black and white tile floor,
checkered curtains, Coca Cola dishes.
Slender waitresses in tight jeans–
mother and daughter, surely–
furnish service and conversation.
Savor Kansas hospitality.

TOURIST FATIGUE

The fields, the ditch, the sky were white
as I drove, quite oblivious to sleepiness.

Five hundred miles from home mid-afternoon
I felt immune to incident I had not meant.

Spouse eased the wheel from my slack hand.
You understand he saved our lives for other drives.

FULFILLING BREAKFAST

Hands twitching, legs jerking, a slight,
loud, restless man speaks in profanities
we cannot help hearing.
His companion listens, drinks his coffee.
The Amish waitress clears their booth.

An older couple settle in, bow, fold
their hands, pray briefly, silently,
add a dimension to my enjoyment
of fried mush, a food I'd enjoyed as a child
when we always bowed our heads.

RURAL IOWA

Twelve-row planters behind green tractors
cover acres an hour on black soil
disced and dragged, go relentlessly
back and forth into night like zoo animals
pacing in pens.

Lush grass in ditches sways except
where farmers mow before their homes–
mostly new or remodeled houses
on yards squared off with groves
of varied varieties in rows of graduated heights.

Gone are native stands of cottonwood
where children raked leaves for outlines
of playhouses, where two-holers were.

No horses pull equipment, get rubbed down,
watered and fed. No windmills turn
to bring water up to be carried in buckets.
No chickens scratch in yards
nor do drying clothes flap from lines.
Few ropes hang from trees with tires attached;
swings are metal with slides beside.

Pieplant flourishes some places,
but they call it rhubarb now.

OUTLINE OF A VACATION

From midwest to west through USA by car
  We see
    Flora
      Wild flowers
        Yellow, pink, white, purple, orange
        Clustered in ditches
        Covering mountainsides
        In pineapple-shaped bunches on cacti
      Cacti
        Tree-shaped, eight feet tall
        Spidery, with long tentacles
        Brown stumps with fingers of new growth
    Fauna
      Antelope graze in New Mexico
      Seals lounge in Pacific
      Jackrabbits lope in Texas
      Sandhill cranes migrate through Nebraska
    Oil Wells
      Pumping monotonously
      Inert, capped or non-producing
    Bridges
      Over rivers and streams
      Over "washes" with no water
      Over rail tracks and other bridges
    Cowboy Hats
      On truck drivers
      On businessmen
      On tourists
      And sometimes on cowboys
  We experience
    Greetings
      Ma'am or Sir
      Y'all or Honey
    Traffic
      Eight lanes zoom in California
      Two lanes mozy through Kansas
  We return home
    To rootedness
    To familiarity
    To wonder if corn and bean fields
      seem strange to them

AFTER VACATION

Light and shadow
through limbs and leaves
pass over my face
this first morning in my own bed
after several states in three weeks
at motels and guest rooms of kin.

Familiar things and sounds surround me.
My clock and bathroom door
are where I expect them to be,
cottonwood tree fluff floats
like errant snowflakes,
robins chirp, a train whistle sounds—
neighbor's wind chime sings.

Mountains that contain minerals,
rivers we would call streams,
sagebrush I thought worthless
that sustains wildlife,
six and eight-lane highways,
buffalo, elk, long-horned sheep
are already memories.

I rise to bake a lemon pie
from hand-picked California fruit,
replace comb and brush, toothpaste,
clothing and shoes in their places,
saunter around our house
bordered by lilacs and oak trees.
Not a palm tree in sight.

NORTH TO ALASKA

CROSS INTO CANADA

"Arret" (Stop, to us)
A few questions at customs
and we are free to go.

Sign says: "Welcome to Alberta,
Wild Rose Country;" the welcome
 hearty from individuals as well.
Trucker explains this is the "Banana Belt,"
with weather warmer than Minnesota

We lose our way in Calgary,
city with far-reaching suburbs,
theaters, culture centers,
banks, business offices;
find long, straight roads
undulating between birch and fir,
past lumber kilns.

White-painted fences and lilacs
surround village homes.
Red Maple Leaf flags fly
at public places, remind us
we are foreigners here.

UNIVERSALITY OF RURAL LIFE

It seems one might walk
on the sea of wheat,
the carpet of yellow canola.

Farmers come and go at a long table
in small town's only café,
shake for coffee, mention dry weather.
"I'll cut hay tomorrow," one says.
"That'll bring rain," is the response.

MILEPOST ZERO

Heading for Alaska, park
at the Information Center
at Dawson Creek for photo-op
at Mile Zero of Alaska Highway.
Dodge traffic to stand at a monument
in center of an intersection
before historic Alaska Hotel with a pub
right out of John Wayne movies.
GIs built the road in eight months
during WWII, a route
to military bases in Alaska

Restored grain elevator,
painted red, displays local art.
Blue Goose Caboose,
a remodeled railroad car,
offers ice cream cones to lick
as we head to "Seward's Folly."

DRIVE IN THE MOUNTAINS

Roadside sign does not encourage;
states, "Avalanche area. Do not stop."

Rocky sides do appear they might slide
onto road on this ledge above valley far below.
We hurry on.

UPSIDE-DOWN AND BACKWARD

In Alpine-like mountains
clouds are below us.
Though June, snow plops
on windows fogging over.
Whitewater rushes "uphill;"
our heads know better.
Tarmac ahead appears to descend;
motor sound insists we climb.
We go to bed at 11:30
and it is light outside.

27

MOUNTAINS, RIVERS, FORESTS

Bridge over Kiskatinaw River
spans deep crevice.
Tall, slender birch and polar
so thick they grow foliage only at top
line highways.

Seven and nine-percent grades
descend and curve
until only the compass knows
which way we go.

Sign announces,
"Caution, Moose on Highway."
We see none ahead, but one in a pond.
Above clouds at Summit Lake,
water, green from glaciers, sparkles.

Beyond Toad River, pines grow up rocky slope.
Perpendicular face above
rises to where spindly trees line the top.

Black bears saunter in ditches,
wildflowers adapted to short summers
flaunt jaunty yellow, pink, purple blooms,
float planes take off and land on Laird River.

Boardwalk leads to hot springs smelling sulfur.
Ferns, wild roses, bluebells, thimbleberry grow,
and fish acclimated to warm water swim.

Nature reclaims hillsides with undergrowth
where fire felled scarred, limbless pines
on four-hundred thousand acres of mountains.

Watson Lake features an unnatural forest
of signposts pointing to cities everywhere
hammered to twelve-foot posts six deep
and a block long, started by a homesick G.I.
tacking his home town's name to a post.

"2,000 FRIENDLY PEOPLE"

Most of them line Main Street
in Souris to watch.
Waitress at coffee shop
says it starts soon so we stay.
Typical of small town parades,
kids with plastic bags run out
to retrieve candy thrown
from fire trucks, floats, tractors.

"Longest Swinging Bridge"
another sign states.
We walk through town
to find it, feel queasy crossing.
It bounces with each step,
prompts me to hold steel railing
chest high beside me.

Rather than two-mile walk
to solid bridge, we retrace our steps;
I, close behind spouse, match step for step
and the bounce is gone.

Perhaps life is like that.
Walk in tandem with mate,
smooth out the rough spots.
Take time to stop and interact
with other friendly people.

PERSPECTIVE

In an elephant of a bus, tires
taller than a man, we lumber
down a 32 degree slope to ice-age
glacier a thousand feet thick.

Drinkable meltwater will flow
to Pacific, Atlantic, Arctic
for centuries after
we forty fly-sized creatures
have left this place.

ROADSIDE CHARACTER

Grizzled, skinny, mustached man
stands stripping bark
from burled spruce trunks
of various length and girth.

He finds and harvests them in spring
when sap flows and the stripping
comes easy, then lets them age.
"The wood has more character
after it is aged, just like people,"
he says as we view his display
of hand-crafted furniture.

"I do this long hours in summer.
Most people sit in bars
and get drunk evenings in winter–
I go home to my family."
Tells of marriage to Indian girl,
with 18-month-old baby.

Down the road we see a burled trunk,
appreciate its uniqueness, and his.

FOR THE FUTURE

Trees are felled first one side,
then the other in preparation
for straightening the road.
Man in ten-ton Caterpillar leans
to right instinctively, ineffectively,
driving at fifteen degree slant.

Pilot car leads through construction.
Orange ribbons on surveyors' tripods
point out the plan.

Water trucks fill from creeks
to wet down graveled roads
though today rain is making
the process moot.

FLATLANDER'S VACATION

We travel through Yukon in month of June
in awe of vastness, snow-capped mountaintops
to lake of emerald green with pines beside
tenacious as they set their roots in rocks.

Fresh water tumbles down beside the road
and flows to find its home in glacial lake.
Old silver mines, abandoned, beckon stops
where tourists' lenses lock the scene in place.

Their dandelions grow carnation size;
bright pansy faces smile from window box.
Roadside a spiky purple flower blooms
as well as other species we can't name.

They snapped my picture standing by rhubarb
as tall as I with succulent red stalks.
In fall the tended gardens will abound
with cabbages that weigh a hundred pounds.

EXPLORE THE YUKON

Tranquil lakes welcome white swans with cygnets.
Green steel bridges span wide, flat rivers (as dry
as the Platte) that were wide and rushing in April.
No Name Creek is dry, though snow
still rests in mountain crevices.

Clouds peek over peaks like white nurses' caps.
Blackened skeletons of burnt firs
with scant undergrowth tell of former fires.
Low-growing grasses and wildflowers bloom.

MOUNTAIN TRAVEL MODES

Senior Citizens' F-150 pickup
valiantly pulls RV through mountains
of tough Sam McGee country.
Young persons in shorts
hike and bike, carry backpacks.

HAINES, ALASKA

Short gravel runway for bush pilots
parallels the road.
Bald Eagle Preserve shows
not an eagle our day there.
Orange-jacketed whitewater riders
tumble downriver in rubber rafts
that do not look safe.

Along river's edge, a paddle-wheel-
like contraption scoops up salmon.
Another place, DNR person counts
salmon swimming in controlled spots.

Fourth of July, the parade
is very like ours at home.
Teens and young adults play volleyball
barefoot on a muddy court
wetted down yesterday.
Children in firemen's hats and slickers
aim fire hoses at buoy slung on
a long rope above and between them.

Winding driveways lead to private homes
lakeside, not visible from the road
in Chilkat State Park forest.
Be sure to stop at Chilkat Bakery
for coffee and a bear claw when you go.

UNPLANNED WORSHIP

I walk to a hilltop
on Sunday morning
thousands of miles from home.
Organ music, where no church
nor organist is, fills the quiet.
The Lord's Prayer follows.
I wonder at the source
of this amplification,
but do not need to know.

ONE MUST DO IT

It is not like there is anything there.
Well, other than a sign
that says, "Arctic Circle."

Wait for road construction
near an outcropping of rock
named Finger Mountain
prompts a walk to the top.
Tundra topography–
weedy grasses, scrubby bushes.
Placards on stakes
identify plucky wild flowers.

Alaska pipeline follows the road,
sometimes underground,
sometimes above.

Six adults in two-seated pickup
drive four hundred miles, round trip
on bad roads, are shaken, tired,
disappointed not to see wildlife.
A huge hamburger alfresco
at "Hot Spot" north of Fairbanks
is worth telling about, and we can say
we went to the Arctic Circle.

PARADOX OF MIDNIGHT SUN

"What time is it?" I asked a man
in California, years ago.
"I really could not say," he said.
"I have no use for watches now.
When I awake, I raise my shade.
If it is light, I know it's day,
and if it's dark, it must be night
and that is all I need to know."
Alaska tourists in mid-June,
we try to go to sleep at night,
but it is light as day outside
and we, two seniors, just as he
cannot rely on his (what seemed
a very good) philosophy.

RUDE AWAKENING

If the monotony of fir and pine
alongside for miles and miles
does nothing else
it reminds us, if we are
full of ourselves,
that there is a lot of world
out there that neither knows
nor cares
that we exist.

VARIED ECONOMY

Western Saskatchewan is dry.
Canola should be waist high, measures inches.
John Deere and IH dealers display tractors
and harvesters, are edgy as the farmers.

Truckloads of hay go north to ranchers
whose Angus and Charolais exist on
sage-colored pastures, drying waterholes.
Clouds overhead refuse to release rain.

Farther east, rain spatters the windshield
cattails thrive in ditches, ducks settle on ponds.
Groves in precise rows on north sides
of homesteads protect white houses,
red barns, multiple grain bins.

Villages boast huge grain elevators,
grain trains a half-mile long.
Black-eyed susans border the road.
Lakes of blue-blossomed flax
beside carpets of yellow canola
thrive along with wheat.

It hardly seems fair that, scattered
among lush fields, oil rigs are pumping.

PEACE GARDENS

Experience a spiritual lift
at the Peace Chapel.
Fountain trickles water
and organ plays hymns,
background to walking
the perimeter, reading quotes
from the Bible, Buddhism
and famous persons reflecting
on philosophies of peace and love,
the whole a monument
to the fact there has never been,
nor shall there ever be,
war between Canada and America;
especially poignant to Minnesotans
after five weeks away
traveling freely across Canada
to Alaska, and back through
the provinces to re-enter U.S.A.
at this place.

ALTERED VIEW OF NORTH DAKOTA

Stories of "Dust Storm Years"
had convinced me North Dakota
would be dry and sere.
Fickle nature drops showers
on Devils Lake where locals
elevate roads, bridges and levees
to prevent flooding,
but fields nearby are arid.

Optimistic farmers plant small plots
on level places and up sidehills,
carry small stones to tops of mounds
then plow around them
and around rocks too heavy to move.

A rain shower as we pass through
makes the irrigation mechanism
insignificant today.

TO THE SUNSHINE STATE

THEIR SPRING AND OURS

We've had enough of winter snow.
The calendar says it will go–
not soon enough to suit us, though.
A day that makes us think of spring
precedes a day we have to bring
the shovel out. Snowman is king.
Grandchildren think that it is cool
(not cold, but neat) if they miss school
for snow the day of April Fool.

We pack suitcases, drive away;
hear weather forecasts so we may
avoid bad weather where we stay.
Head south to where the soil is brown
far off from blue-black of our town,
to where the road climbs up, goes down;
to where highway snakes into curves
and dropoff without guardrail serves
to hasten heart rate, stretch our nerves.

Observe white-pillared porches–stone
and many-colored brick homes known
to set the ambiance and tone
for us. We're unaccustomed to
homes built primarily for view
of folk who come for just a few
days yearly. They don't have to take
a trip to fish in their own lake–
it's right below them when they wake.
A blacktop lane on mountain crest
that twists and undulates will test
the mettle of a timid guest.

Look off to right or left and see
right at eye-level, top of tree,
and redbuds blooming randomly
at roadsides and across the way
throughout the wooded hills that lay
below, beside us one whole day.
We glimpse the very birthing of
the dogwoods white as turtledove
that legends say tell of His love.
With no leaf yet, the blossom clings
to slender twigs that seem like wings
outspread to hold the tender things.

This Ozark beauty casts a spell;
redbud and dogwood bloom to tell
us spring is here and all is well.
When we turn north, we'll realize
that tulips, lilacs advertise
the same at home just for our eyes.

OZARK DESTINY

Rustling leaves whisper
on valley floor,
converse with ripple of water
begun as trickle, now lake.

Tall, slender trees
hold twig-fingers to hearts
as neighbors on upper slopes
are felled to make way
for foundations of stone,
mortar and brick.

Hammer and saw
obliterate birdsong
that humans may sit on porches
to enjoy the view
that may not be there
if others continue
to fell trees to make way
for foundations of stone,
mortar and brick.

INVINCIBLE AS THE MOUNTAIN

Somehow surveyed,
plotted and numbered,
thousands of acres
in Ozark Mountains
are meccas
for persons retired
or seeking transport
from schedules, desks
and telephones.

Each property has personality–
grand or practical
depending upon the owner–
windows for viewing,
patios for grilling,
sheds for golf carts,
gardens for flowers.

But none is so singular
nor defiant
as the plot developers
could not purchase,
where no amount of money
would move the mountain woman
who will stay till her death
in tin-roofed, patched-together home
surrounded by chickens, pigs,
a few petunias and a couple rusty Buicks,
fulfilling her destiny.

TO EXPERIENCE "OTHER"

Tourists vie for place on inadequate streets,
find lodging, stay a day or week. Roads
wind around to palaces, museums, theaters.
Billboards praise dancers, comedians, musicians.
Pleasure-seekers file down aisles behind
tour guides with flags. At least two shows
per day will sate the hunger for "different."

HOW OTHERS LIVE

Towns five blocks wide and five miles long
lie bisected by freeways through the hollers.
Homes tucked halfway up mountains
will be invisible once trees are leafed.
Interspersed among tight-foliaged cedars,
wispy redbuds flourish wildly
on multi-layered ledges where mountains
have been hacked back for access.

Headstones cover whole hillsides adorned
with flowers; other places two or three
crosses on private ground.

A blue Ford tractor turns brown soil
on small, irregularly-shaped plots
with tobacco sheds behind.
On the next knoll, white fences surround
a red-brick, white-pillared home
on landscaped acres.

Yellow lines split highways in thirds,
two lanes uphill, one down.
Signs announce deer, fallen rock,
"Horse Capitol of the World."

We feel transported to another land.
Towns named Paris, Versailles, Frankfort
underscore the illusion.

HORSE COUNTRY

West of Lexington, black fences form
islands around trees, border rectangles
of green dotted with sleek-backed mares
with colts beside, slender-legged
and sorrel-maned as young women.

Pastures wave various-colored grasses.
On the hill, dimension and grandeur
of house and paddock attest to
the excellence of horses and equestrians.

KENTUCKY COAL

It lies in piles near railroad tracks,
is striated in hillsides
sliced through for freeways,
slivers off onto roadside;
black as the briquettes
Dad once fed our parlor heater,
as the smoke our chimney emitted.

Heavy-duty trucks full of it
lumber around mountain roads,
emit diesel exhaust.
Heavy-duty men go into earth's bowels,
come out with black lung.

Loretta Lynn, born of it,
sings of it.

A FEW MILES IN VIRGINIA

Highway 32 drops steeply into Virginia
where we drive only long enough for impressions
and comparisons with Kentucky.

Tall slender trees thickly wood hillsides,
punctuated with wildflowers.
Mountains rise higher, though less severely.
Narrow, tarred roads lead
to homes on ledges halfway up.
Low spots are wider, afford larger lawns,
support scattered herds of angus.

A median thick with red and yellow tulips
splits the lanes in one place.
Coal cars black as their cargo laze
silently on a siding near a high trestle.
Gullies filled with stones ward off erosion.

An elderly couple picnic at a table between
the Daniel Boone Heritage Trail and a stream.

A TASTE OF TENNESSEE

Rain pounds, requires high-speed wipers
that mesmerize, swish plops of moisture,
then is done. We wind through hazy Smokies
more rolling than mountainous.
Signposts rise high to assure
food, gas, restaurants around next bend.

Felled trees on a hillside make way
for power lines to march up and over.
Green grass and budded trees
belie Februaryness to Yankees.

Grits and biscuits and gravy
at Shoneys, Steak n Bake, Bob Evans
are not the treats they once were
as those eateries move ever northward.

A CORNER OF NORTH CAROLINA

Roadside oak branches mingle
above our two-lane road,
though we see construction
for future freeway.

On a 9% grade downhill
a cement truck traveling 25 mph,
we passed earlier before stopping,
delays us.

Nude gray branches
among pines on ridges
beg one imagine fall colors.
At lower elevations, most deciduous
show mustard-green leaf-beginnings.
Tall trees grow densely with leaves
only at the top, resemble lollipops,
are called loblolly pines.
As we gape at unfamiliar sights,
white golf carts follow paths
to a brick clubhouse.

41

SHOCKING THE SENSES

We leave Minnesota, ascend into flight,
the cold, snowy crispness smelling of white.

Of beverage offered before we touch down,
we choose cups of coffee, inhaling the brown;

depart Tampa's airport, arrive on this scene:
a man mowing roadsides–the scent's very green.

HOW THE OTHER HALF LIVE IN FLORIDA

They shore up inlets, build homes
with sailboats moored beside,
landscape with palm trees, bougainvillea, hibiscus
on islands reached by crossing drawbridges.
Condominiums vie for sky space.

Many-windowed, multi-colored, trendy shops
provide food, clothing, jewelry, bric-a brac
on streets named Flamingo, Heron, Hummingbird.
They house Renaults, Lincolns, Mercedes
in three-car garages with painted driveways.

We recross the bridge, go to public beaches,
pick up seashells.

GEORGIA INTERSTATE

Three lanes beyond median head for paradise
we lately left–seashore, palm trees, pelicans.
Iowa, New York, Michigan cars, trucks, Rvs
pass on either side. Traffic does not slow them
nor do hills or wayside beauty.

Even we, retired folk who stop sometimes
at antique places, are determined
to be back to home and snow
by Saturday.

DRIVER'S WISDOM

He overrides my Type A
desire for efficiency,
for zooming through or around
metropolis and suburbs
on six-lane highways
past Hilton Hotels
and Cadillac dealerships.

We meander red-line roads
without shoulders,
up and down hills,
around curves,
through narrow bridges;
to see men on small tractors
turn brick-red soil,
dairy cows with calves in pastures,
tall cement grain elevators
and John Deere equipment
lined up like green dominoes.

Slowing to 30 mph and stopping
at small towns and burgs,
we sleep in Super 8s,
dine at Mom and Pop Cafes,
converse with local farmers,
enjoy their, "C'mon back, y'all."

Retired, we really need not speed;
enjoy domed courthouses,
white wooden churches with spires,
old houses with front porches,
businesses with church pews
out front for lollygagging–
all hugging the roadway
because a mountain or a holler
is behind them with
wild fruit trees blooming
and daffodils in ditches.

FEBRUARY TRAVELS

Designated co-pilot,
I sat with map on lap
through eleven states
to transplanted kin and friends.

One-and-a-half days of sunshine
in three weeks did not dismay us.
Sun-worship was not our cause.

Florida cousin renewed vows.
Eighty-year-old brother
took us to seafood place,
showed us his RV park.

We celebrated our anniversary,
met sister's infant grandchildren,
watched manatees in a cove,
toured Tampa Bay
ate at Amish restaurants,
walked on white gulf sand,
picked up shells.

On return trip, back seat
contained oranges, grapefruit,
pecans, antiques, gifts.

After two-day drive to Kentucky
through coal country, we visited
another brother, overate.
In the Ozarks, friends dealt bridge cards,
helped us find collectibles.

A good trip,
though our photo album is in Sanford,
his corduroy vest in the Amish restaurant
and my pillow in a Kentucky motel.

WHEN MIGRANTS RETURN

Oblivious, we knew the kiss of sun
while blizzards and an ice storm raged at home.
So often were we told of our good luck
and how the others had to shovel, just
to get to work, to school. We did, indeed,
enjoy our sojourn there, the fruit, the feel
of salt spray foreign to our skin. Seashells
along the beach invited us to help
ourselves. We picked them up. Our eyes took in
the strangeness of the palms, the twining fingers
of the unfamiliar vines. The moss that looped
and hung from trees seemed odd to Ykankees. Roomed
with southern kin, we had the fortune to
be chauffeured here and there and told the rules
of nature that affected growth. We soon
just took for granted seeing trees in bloom,
the pink hibiscus, size of dinner plates,
and brightly plumaged birds we could not name.

Once home, we readjusted to the cold
and found about the yard the sticks and whole
bare limbs the ice had broken down; no bloom
to brighten black against the snow. And truth
be known, regret is in our hearts, for we
were told that while the ice encrusted each
and every limb and twig on our lawn's oaks
our neighbor stepped outside her door, and oh!
The morning sun upon the sleeted sprouts
produced prismatic rainbows all about;
the tinkling, chiming sound the breezes made
was like a choir, and we were far away.

TO NEW ENGLAND AND BEYOND

BUILDING MEMORIES

I prepare grilled cheese sandwiches and tomato soup
in RV backed onto sand dune of Lake Superior,
cut up a New Zealand apple
as tape purchased from street player in London
emits haunting flute music,
apropos of this windswept beach.

Three weathered, broken tugs, long in disuse,
surrounded by ropes thicker than my arm
looped over posts upright in sand
give impression of dry dock.

Lone boat on horizon floats beneath white sail.
Waves curl onto shore in ruffled whitecaps,
disturb mallards foraging there.
Backpacker saunters by.
Small, white butterfly hovers.

I remove a single candy wrapper from seascape
before snapping close-up of yellow yarrow
that blooms everywhere.

Boat-filled marina and restaurant
are main enterprises, but we saunter
through century-old houses, now shops,
that offer used books, cold drinks,
popcorn, white elephants, antiques.

I purchase a green bowl
in my pattern of depression glass,
will see this place each time I use it.

OFF THE FREEWAY

Purple, white and yellow wildflowers
that farmers likely label weeds
abound in ditches along with sumac.

Jagged limestone bluffs jut out
where roads cut through;
tarred two-lanes wind up, down
and around hills, forests,
the Little Sugar and Baraboo Rivers.

Holsteins graze in pastures
where barns dominate the landscape;
big barns surrounded by silos
on manicured dairy farms,
small, weathered barns, tin roofs
rusting at abandoned places.

Patches of hay or corn grow
on stingy flat spaces.
Trees or swamp cut into
irregularly-shaped fields.
On larger expanses,
various crops wrap around
hillsides like corduroy
in parallel tiers, inhibit erosion.
Hay lays in windrows
or round bales wrapped in plastic.

Detours force slower pace,
heighten appreciation.

EXPERIENCE A FISH BOIL

Guests sit on benches,
watch them stoke blazing wood fires
beneath iron kettles
lined with wire baskets.
They fling handfuls of salt
into boiling water,
add scrubbed new potatoes, onions,
and, later, whitefish.

When tested done,
a little kerosene in the fire
produces flashes of flames
Scummy water boils over sides.

Two men grasp the pole
through basket handles,
carry it inside.
Guests stand in line,
wait for plates to be served
with slaw and dark-brown bread
beside butter-smothered
potatoes, onions, fish
with wedges of lemon.

Waitresses bring coffee or tea,
keep cups filled.
Choice of cherry or apple pie
tops off the Door County, Wisconsin
phenomenon.

WHEELERS

Teenagers pedal past
as we rest,
read markers, interpret maps,
take great gulps of air.

We walk cycles up inclines,
ride single file
when meeting fellow bikers
or horse-drawn carriages;

stop to snap pictures,
ask directions,
gratefully coast
on downhill stretches...

four almost-senior citizens
deny paunches and graying hair,
bicycle across
Mackinac Island.

SOURCE AND USE

Miniature Eiffel Towers
strung together with cable
march across mountain and prairie
in lines straight as an honor guard,
carry power.

Somewhere a waterfall,
nuclear plant
or coal-burning furnace
has produced electricity.

A hundred miles away
a mother puts a pan of brownies
into an oven.

FISHERMEN AT HEART

On six-lane bridge
full of potholes,
with sun in our eyes
and vehicles traveling
maniacal speeds
weaving in and out,
we decide
the only one who's sane
is that fellow out there
in the boat.

ILLINOIS OIL

We appreciate their agriculture.
Wide, flat fields, long, straight
corn rows offset by winter wheat
surround manicured dooryards.

Awkward looking rig heads
rise and fall, draw oil
so they may harvest
below ground, as well.

RUSTIC OR FAMILIAR?

Covered bridges and old mills
draw vacationers from freeways.
Most charming are those
that are weathered–

boards blue-gray,
fieldstone foundations
held together more by placement
than what is left of mortar.

Vines rooted in yesterday
find fingerholds,
climb rough sides,
send tendrils through cracks.

We thrill to sounds
of water flowing, wheel creaking;
smell mustiness of years,
see reflections in stream.

Ingenuity and craftsmanship
placed timbers across a span,
lifted shafts and gears
of great weight into place.

Pictures of horses drawing carriages
of folk through bridges
and wagons of wheat to mills
enter our consciousness.

Once, at edge of our town,
we saw a family
with out-of-state license plates
snapping pictures of a field of corn.

IF IT HAD NOT STORMED

As if plows had turned back,
ice-packed roads stretch ahead.
Cars, pickups, semis, a motorhome
litter ditches and median.
Nine miles of westbound vehicles
wait, immobile. Wreckers
 in left lane allow advance by spurts.

We exit first ramp, buy fuel
at a truck stop, converse with couple
who note our Minnesota license.
We identify our home town–
where they interviewed last week.
A pastor, he will serve the parish
where I sing in choir.

Six hundred miles from home begins
a relationship destined to become
more than just shepherd/flock.

FIRST TRIP ON MASSACHUSETTS TURNPIKE

With touches of bronze and red,
Berkshire hills, mostly green, invite us.
The road appears to have grown unaided
along with flora until we notice
where it was cloven through rocks.

Sumac and goldenrod push against
retaining fences, strain toward tourists, truckers.
Clear streams weave about, water for deer,
unseen except painted on signs that warn
they might dart onto roadways.
At less than two thousand feet we are at apex,
advises sign with Pilgrim hat logo.

I appreciate guardrails, do not resent
road construction, silently thank tanned workers
perspiring so that I, usually white-knuckled
in mountains, might delight in landscaped medians.
vistas over crest of every hill.

QUESTIONS ABOUT A MOLLUSK

Washed onto shore, a spiraled shell
casts but a tiny shadow.
Wound round and round
as thread on a spool, white
speckled with brown, the shell
is smooth, hard mysterious.

One of thousands of varieties,
shapes and colors, how did
the little critter create this home?
Was it lonesome in there?
Did it know its cousins,
those of the other thousands,
or even its mother and father?
Did other creatures or fishes
admire or antagonize it?
Was its circular house safe
from predators, from atomic bombs?
Could the creature come out to play
and return–wend its way inside?
Did it worry in stormy weather?

Do naturalists know these answers?
Have they bothered to ponder
the wonder of the being
that fashioned the seashell
that is smooth, hard and mysterious
in my hand?

FOLLOWING THE ARSONIST

The forest is on fire! Red and orange
tongues dart among green pines.
We catch our breath as twigs
and branches, whole trees submit.
We drive beside, settle back
in seats through areas of green,
then gasp at leafy trees in flame.
We chose this route that we might see it–
not nature consumed, but the epitome
of autumn color in Maine in September.

52

RESPITE IN THE WOODS

Out of breath, I lean against
a rough-sawn rail nailed to cedar trees,
watch the rapids in a wide stream
with reddish-brown rocks,
flat and cracked
where water trickles, roars,
roils, smooths out, flows to a noisy fall.
Others trek to see it closely
while I elect to wait alone,
let water sounds surround me,
watch tree squirrel
hop from branch to twig above,
then down to my eye level.
He chee, chees at me,
tail twitching with every sound.
I mock him, cheeing back.
He stares at me before descending.

Trees at my side, branches bare of needles,
are Christmas-tree perfect at peaks.
Only stream and squirrel
intrude upon the stillness.

Fog obscures the campsite
where owner pointed out a trail
to berries for picking,
and to this view.
Pure luck drew us here, a gem
in the bracelet of our trip through Canada.

They return, we pick up blueberries
left with me, backtrack to our trailers,
and not only our pails are filled.

TWO KINDS OF BEAUTY

We marvel at wooded mountain peaks,
inlets, coves, incoming tides and vistas
where we can see forever.
At least as lovely are wild asters, ragweed,
cattails flourishing in ditches.

53

TROLLEY DRIVER

Young, red haired, good looking,
he is endowed with only two hands
which he uses with dexterity
of octopus, holds microphone
to describe what we are seeing
in both French and English,
points to Quebec attractions,
reaches for chart to keep on schedule;
steers that unwieldy vehicle
down narrow streets and steep hills,
barely misses other traffic,
quips, "Not bad for first-time driver."

He impresses with knowledge
and endearing wit;
in expected French fashion,
punctuates statements
with fling of yet another hand.

CANADA, OUR NEIGHBOR

Crests of gentle hills are vantage points to view valleys,
white houses, spired churches. They forecast temperatures
in twenties and thirties that startle us until we remember
they measure in Celsius. Common there and here—
road construction and Maple Leaf or Stars and Stripes flying.

WEE BIT OF FOREIGN CULTURE

We see a Gaelic School beside the road
and stop our drive along the mountainside
of Nova Scotia's well-toured Cabot trail.
A freckle-faced young lady puffs her cheeks
while moving fingers on the slender rod
of whining bagpipe slung across her back.
She tells of courses offered old and young
in piping, dancing, weaving of the wool
for tartans, afghans, tam-o-shanters, scarves.
We feel the texture of those offerings,
delight in colors woven expertly,
know we have seen a bit of Scotland here
and breathe their phrase. "A hundred thousand thanks."

WORLD TRAVEL

ALTERED FLIGHT

We leave behind
one with a broken wing.
His distraught mate
insisted that we go
though we were meant
to soar as four.

We find and join
compatriots
the same way bound.

We go to trace
the nesting place
of former generations
of the male.

We dry disappointment
from our eyes
and try to swallow guilt
that only we shall see the fjords,
shall tread the ground
where he, too,
had hoped to trace his ancestry.

We vow intensity,
absorbing
everything we see
to bring on our return
bright images.

We take within our hearts
our wounded friend.

TO SLEEP OR NOT TO SLEEP

My spouse, who said he could not sleep in flight
is doing so, while I, who said I could,
sit bolt upright, scan horizon turning gold, pale blue.

Red and white lights blinking at edge of wings
contrast my window view–afar
a star in inky darkness.

Ten twenty-five p.m. My watch defends
his right to sleep as he would do through news
at home in Minnesota, as we descend
through clouds in early morning Copenhagen.

INVENTORY OF MORNING NORWEGIAN CUISINE

Cold fish for breakfast–
in red sauce, creamy sauce, vinegar
Cold meats, thin sliced, arranged on platters
Pickles–cucumber and beet
Great chunks of cheese–
white, yellow, brown
with slicer provided
Water pitchers of milk and orange juice
Soup bowls stored beside cornflakes,
museli, a vegetable bowl of sugar
Baskets or porcelain hens
with nests of soft-boiled eggs
near stacks of egg cups
Pyramid of saucers and cups
beside pots of strong coffee,
hot water for tea
In most hotels, yogurt and fresh fruit–
in some, caviar
Little plastic boxes of smor (butter in English)
vegetable bowls of jam–
strawberry, orange marmalade, and one other
Generous trays of breads–
coarse white, whole wheat, hard crusted buns
that sprinkle crumbs onto the lap
of one who presumes to split them

A SHORT LIFE IN NORGE

I am born a Norwegian in Oslo,
baptized by rain
at King Olaf's palace,
educated by mazes of streets
leading to museums, parks.
I feel kin to Ibsen, Munch and Grieg,
am nurtured by new-found cousins
in the countryside.
I learn awe and trust
weaving, turning,
ascending, descending
from barren peaks
to meadows and barns.
Faith is confirmed
as pastors intone liturgy, scripture
in language I do not know
at church spouse's Grandfather attended.
I feel married to sights, sounds,
tastes, textures of the country,
the kiss of mountain air;
grow old with ferries,
fjords and waterfalls.

I lie awake beneath a feather quilt
as clock demands
the remaining breath
from the life of my stay
in Norway.

REACHING OUT

Comfortable and safe,
the valley,
the foothill
pastoral, serene;

but to fully know
the waterfall
one must be prepared
to ascend the mountain.

57

AUSTRIAN ADVENTURE

With thirty aboard,
the car swoops up
on a ridiculously slim cable,
a ten-foot-square box
    swaying slightly
side to side
    carrying tourists,
some obviously American
others lederhosen-clad natives.

A small nausea builds
as I try to decide
between closed eyes
or viewing mountains,
glaciers, waterfalls.
Near apex, thinking
to exit soon, I peek
at my surroundings.

Our transport rolls
through pulleys at a tower
I thought to be the top,
slacks to another arc
to access higher peak,
causes further angst.

Silent prayer certainly
keeps cable sturdy
to deposit us at summit,
wide-eyed, in a plateau
of ankle-deep meadow grass,
edelweiss and windflowers
among scattered rocks.

The awe is just enough
to give me courage
to re-enter the cable car
for the return trip.

ACROSS THE POND

The mist hangs heavy on the mountaintop.
Quite often, in a day, the raindrops drop
but with umbrella, jacket and a will
I stroll about, absorbing to my fill
the ambience of Ireland, Scotland, Wales
and England in the hillsides and the dales.
The greenness of the grass, the scent of flowers
derived from humid coolness fill my hours.

Much blessed at home with fine community
and friends, associates and family,
I still will often, as these memories fade,
remember strangers smiling, giving aid.
    My storehouse has been filled with sight and sound–
    with British folk I have found common ground.

LIMRICKS WRITTEN IN IRELAND

There once was a tour guide named Kevin,
the year was nineteen ninety-seven.
He told us much lore,
what Guinness is for,
then showed us a wee bit of heaven.

There once was a driver named Bill
who drove up and down every hill,
and around the "S" curves
with strong arms and iron nerves.
I suppose he is doing it still.

Our lassie, named Jenny, you see
in Ireland did not drink the tea.
When she turned twenty-one
we all joined in the fun
and drank to her health in Tralee.

A tour organizer is Gary.
He saw that we all got to Kerry.
He is a fine fella
who lost his umbrella--
He misplaces things? That is scary.

59

I'M ALMOST IRISH NOW

The legends tell of Ireland in poetry and song.
I now have seen old Ireland–my concepts had been wrong.

I stood in awe of castles–how did they build them so
without a crane or mortar a thousand years ago?

Most towns boast a cathedral with spires and leaded glass;
grand courtyards with a railing surrounding verdant grass.

Through gravestones tilting slightly, we walked where nettles grow
in old monastic ruins–Adare and Glendalough.

These relics once were Abbeys with monks, nuns, quiet prayers,
dark, cloistered halls, high turrets, steep, stony winding stairs.

A tourist's jewel, Dublin, with many sights to see–
Halfpenny Bridge, O'Connell Street and College, Trinity

where Medicine and English and Law are some things learned;
where Book of Kells is honored, its artistry discerned.

Sheep, cattle on steep hillsides roam freely, without stall–
corralled by rocky fences resembling China's Wall.

Cool mists hang low on mountains on many days a year
producing right conditions for rainbows to appear.

Fresh flowers, gushing fountains are all about to see;
combining both are gardens–one, named "Rose of Tralee."

Down over rock and pebble the Lee, Avonbeg flow;
clear, winding, through the counties of Kerry, Cork, Wicklow.

Eire's land juts into ocean with sharp, steep rocky coasts.
Shipwrecks of many nations the sea surrounding boasts.

Abundant pubs are noisy with friendly folk, and hale
who gather, seemly, nightly, to quaff a pint of ale.

Hand Bodhran sets the tempo, arm bagpipes wail and sigh–
tin whistle and accordion together make one cry.

Their melodies are mournful, toe dancing, crisp and pert.
You'll not find any Irish who is an introvert.

One has to love their humor, their bon mots and their wit.
Quick sarcasm is gentle. They're quite adept at it.

Wool weavers, deft glass blowers are proud to share their skill.
As they learned from the elders those crafts are practiced still.

A monument or statue immortalizes men
or women worth the honor in many cities' ken.

These people built a nation–are very proud of it–
of rocks, peat, gorse and labor and goodly share of grit.

I've memories of Ireland, her cool and misty dawns,
her castles, streams and rainbows. I near hear leprechauns.

VANISHING LANDSCAPE

Once, threads of hedgerows
stitched fields in Wales together,
kept sheep in clusters,
dairy cows contained.

Modern methods negate
the need to rotate crops,
move flocks and herds
from field to field.

Plots are larger now;
other crops than hay
are cultivated, harvested
with larger machines.

Centuries-old shrub fences
are gone
and some of the romance
is removed
from British landscape.

A BIT OF SCOTLAND

The Vikings, Normans, Romans, Celts
invaded place of glacial melts;
though plundering, in ages past,
built roads and structures that would last.
While they left much esteemed today,
most of that history is gray
with bloodshed, brief-held loyalties
and hostages held past the seas.

Scots suffered much, both high and low
throughout the never-ending flow
of base pretenders to the crown;
were not completely beaten down.

I walked in Scottish town today
and there, down low along the way,
a wee blue flower has had birth
where vagrant seed found bit of earth.
On slender stem, with leaves of green,
like soul of Scotsmen can be seen
between the cobblestones and rock,
survivor in a wispy frock.

KINSHIP WITH THE MASTERS

A bit of lake, just seen between the trees
through window specked with rain is just a tease
that calls me out to view it from the lane,
for I shall likely not pass here again.

The time to love and fully know the lakes
of Coleridge and Wordsworth surely takes
more than a day or two. I must aspire
to know what thrilled them, set their hearts afire.

Stone fences, castles, houses, pastured hills
oak trees, green vines, red roses, daffodils
are much the same as when the bards walked here
along the paths and shores of Windermere.

The verses that were learned in school from books
sing in the sounds of birds and breeze and brooks.

BACK TO SCOTLAND

"The main glen plunged down
a succession of corries and spurs
to the purling waters of a narrow burn."
From <u>September</u> by Rosamunde Pilcher

Lost in descriptions I don't understand,
I feel draughts and mist on my face,
hear streams tumbling,
see kitchens with four-oven Agas.

With unusual turns of phrase,
words like splendid, wee, lochs,
British spellings of pyjamas, labour, favourite
the author paints a tapestry:

> crofts surrounded by hedges
> sheep farms with fences and gates
> estates with drawing rooms
> fireplaces with fenders
> backyards called gardens
> mowed places for croquet
> men in tweeds or kilts
> and cobbled streets in Edinburgh

Curled on my hide-a-bed sofa
(called a Put-U-Up in the book)
I fill in the spaces only imagined
on our miserly two-day pass
through Scotland
on a fifteen day tour of Britain.

TOUCHE

On London's underground train
I see a sign, "Priority Seats,"
tell spouse,
"We are to give up these seats
to the elderly."

His response,
"We are they."

FIRST DAY ON OAHU

Mainlanders refer to maps,
gauge positions by which side
is mountain or ocean,
walk through affluent old hotels
to Waikiki beach
on streets with names full of vowels–
names we cannot pronounce
but roll from tongues of Hawaiians
like music–
watch surfers ride waves,
children build sand castles,
bikini-clad girls saunter.

THE BUS takes us anyplace
to shop, to see a show, to eat.
At International Marketplace,
kiosks offer mumus,
chocolate covered macadamias,
hand-carved hardwood jewelry,
and eateries serve ethnic foods
under banyan trees
with birds scavenging crumbs.

At evening we plan our week–
Arizona Memorial, zoo,
Polynesian Village, a luau,
Punchbowl, volcanic crater–
and vow to remember
sunscreen.

WHY TAKE VACATIONS?

We plan, anticipate,
then escape
the ordinary.

We experience; then, happily,
return home
to remember.